Egon Schiele

Nudes

EGON SCHIELE

Text by Alessandra Comini

RIZZOLI
NEW YORK

in association with
GAGOSIAN GALLERY

Schiele's Nudes: Prurience or Pathos?

BY ALESSANDRA COMINI

As issues of censorship in art once again spark public debate at the end of this century, it is intriguing to recall that the explicitly erotic depiction of female nudes by the Viennese Expressionist artist Egon Schiele (1890–1918) was subject to an extreme form of censorship at the beginning of the century. On a gray day in May, 1912, before a stunned courtroom in the small Austrian town of St. Pölten, a provincial judge chastised the twenty-one-year-old artist for his "immorality," as proved by the subject matter of several confiscated drawings. The judge then solemnly held one of the drawings over a candle flame, setting it ablaze. Ironically, the magistrate who condemned Schiele was an avid collector of the works of a mentally unbalanced painter priest Franz Stecher (1814–1853), whose images were murky mixtures of sexual and religious elements, *à la* William Blake.[1]

It was just such glaring hypocrisy, with its brittle, multi-faceted facade of propriety, that Schiele wished to shatter. "I do not deny it: I have made drawings and watercolors that are erotic. But they are still always works of art."[2] Schiele's ruthlessly candid and exhibitionist erotic drawings of himself and others are not only "always works of art," due to the artist's trenchant mastery of reductive volume and line, but also audacious darts hurled at the operetta world of aging Kaiser Franz Josef's senescent "City of Dreams"—Vienna. A contemporary of Sigmund Freud, Arnold Schönberg, Oskar Kokoschka, Adolf Loos, Karl Kraus, and Ludwig Wittgenstein, Schiele joined in that collective pursuit of "truth" which the new century brought to bear in the escapist capital of a disintegrating Austro-Hungarian Empire. The inexorable march toward the abyss of World War I, triggered by the seething social and political tensions of the multi-national Habsburg Empire (which have come to a boil again today in the breakup of Yugoslavia), was paralleled in the arts and science by a relentless unmasking of taboos.

Schiele's self-assigned mission—to expose the psyche—mirrored the disturbing new contention that the ugly is beautiful, but his preoccupation was also rooted in personal experience. As a boy he had watched with bewilderment the syphilitic deterioration of his father, who died insane when Schiele was fourteen. Brooding on the venereal genesis of his father's illness promoted a precocious and obsessive fascination for sexuality. Before his full-length mirror, he rapaciously explored himself and others—including his younger sister, and later his sexual partners—confronting with the white magic of his artist's crayon the black magic of sexual desire. None of Schiele's drawings of erotica, whether the racked, revelatory watercolor images of 1910 or the coolly distant, voyeuristic black chalk figures of 1918, are ever joyful. They are unflinching documentations of human flesh flushed with desire. Purples, Venetian reds, and oranges highlight tumescent lips, nipples, and genitals; black angular lines hack out contorted contours, amputate extremities, and concentrate on writhing torsos. By coming to grips with the sexual imperative, Schiele was mastering not only it but—for him—its twin: death.

The mirthless intensity of this procedure is cogently captured in the artist's virtuoso pencil drawing of 1910, *Self-Portrait Seated with Standing Nude Female Model.* With successsive diminutions in size, the mirror reflects what is nearest the artist: the model's figure from the back, then her figure from the front, and, finally, the artist with his drawing-board gazing at what the mirror reveals. His lips are pursed, his forehead is furrowed, and one eye narrows (*schielen* = "to squint," the artist's secret "signature") in total concentration.

The assemblage of matching points such as shoulders, elbows, wrists, and knees is as stunningly intricate in alignment as it is seemingly facile in execution. An eyewitness account tells us how Schiele worked: "The sureness of his hand was almost infallible. When drawing he most often sat on a low footstool, the drawing-board with its paper on his knees, and the right hand with which he drew propped on a support....An eraser was unknown to him."[3] This highly charged velocity, set down at collision speed, endows Schiele's drawings of nudes with a smoldering intensity that is pronounced, arresting, and inescapable.

The speed of execution to which all accounts attest was a potent factor in Schiele's exploration of sexual urgency; unusual perspective was another. By positioning his models on a low mattress set on the floor and viewing them from above, the artist could obtain results that were both shockingly specific and disturbingly ambiguous (a technique that would be imitated by Robert Mapplethorpe in his photographic close-ups). Frequently the artist compounded the confusion by placing his signature so as to enforce a vertical (standing) reading of a horizontal (recumbent) motif. In addition, the empty, monochromatic space in which the artist consistently placed his female nudes (as well as his own nude self-portraits) acts not only to intensify but to suggest an allegorical void. This emphasis on the angst-fraught nil underscores the Expressionist passage (in all the arts) from the environmental to the existential, from the rational to the irrational, and from the facade to the psyche.

Does Schiele's piquant and titillating manipulation of his female nudes constitute what might nowadays be construed as a sexist, "paintbrush as penis" mentality? Certainly many of Schiele's female nudes, especially the pubescent girls and lesbian couples, were created for prurient patrons who subsidized the impecunious young artist and who requested just such "naughty" works.

But Schiele's prurience was of a different cast: it was linked to a grimly earnest preoccupation with death and sexuality. Rather than banish it from his own life, he embraced it, not complicitly as a flesh-and-blood partner (although he did have abundant relationships with the opposite sex and married into a bourgeois family), but as an artist who, exactly because he *was* an artist, had the right, the obligation, to mention the unmentionable, to reveal the "ugly" beautiful truth, to expose the pulsating psyche that had too long been suffocated by society's oppressive facade

of manners and morals. What the physician-turned-playwright Arthur Schnitzler had slyly exposed with the scalpel of his cutting comedy of sexual mores, *Reigen* (*La Ronde*, 1896), Schiele would directly address as primary visual motif in his drawings of nudes.

"Have adults forgotten how corrupted, that is, incited and aroused by the sex impulse they themselves were as children?...I have not forgotten, for I suffered terribly under it," wrote Schiele, recalling the pathos of his troubled adolescence.[4] One of the traumas relentlessly addressed in the early sexual monodramas of 1910 and 1911 was that of masturbation. Paralleling the then commonly-held belief that indulgence in the "solitary vice" could lead to insanity, Schiele's flushed self-images are ridden with guilt, revealing a half-crazed victim of compulsion. Symbolic punishment is dealt out by compositional amputation of arms and lower extremities, while the emotion-racked features and torsos are flecked with acrid colors. The inescapable sexual gene-

INSET: SELF-PORTRAIT SEATED WITH STANDING NUDE FEMALE MODEL, 1910.

sis of such thematic narcissism (with its attendant therapeutic ventilation) even wrested from Schiele's ubiquitous mirror an eerie Doppelgänger—an evil second self who urged the numbed artist into involuntary acts of self-gratification (*The Self-Seers I*, 1910, oil; *The Prophet*, 1911, oil). Not until he had repeatedly cast himself in the roles of lover and, eventually, husband and father (*The Family*, 1917–18, oil), would the twin specters of Eros and death quit the twenty-eight-year-old artist's side. But by then it was too late. The raging influenza that broke out during the last months of World War I took him, his young wife, and their unborn first child all within a few days in October, 1918. The immediacy of Schiele's courageous and unsettling encounter with sexuality endures.

1.   See Alessandra Comini, *Schiele in Prison*, 1973, p. 92.
2.   *Ibid*, p. 58.
3.   Heinrich Benesch, as quoted in Alessandra Comini,
      Egon Schiele's Portraits, 1974, (reissued 1990), p. 64.
4.   *Schiele in Prison*, p. 59.

NUDES

1. MOTHER AND CHILD, 1909.

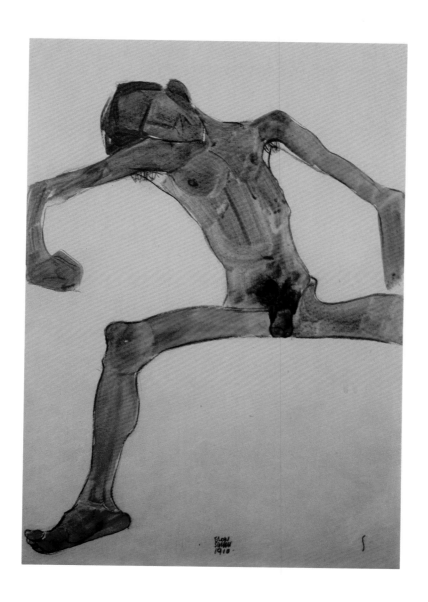

2. KNEELING GIRL, DISROBING, 1910.
3. SEATED MALE NUDE, 1910.

4. NEWBORN BABY, 1910.

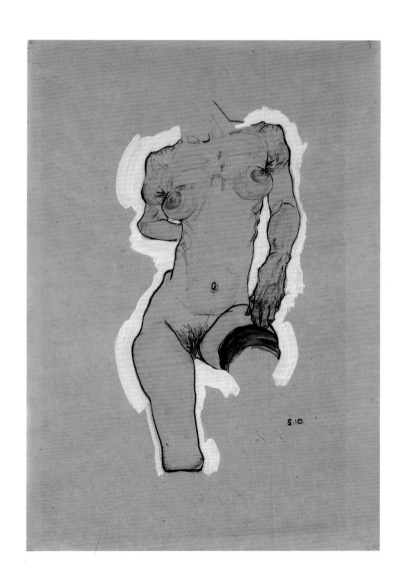

5. STANDING NUDE, BACK VIEW, 1910.
6. FEMALE TORSO, 1910.

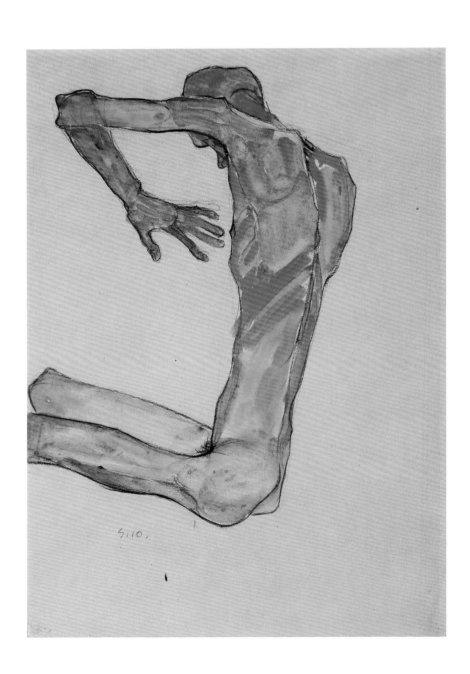

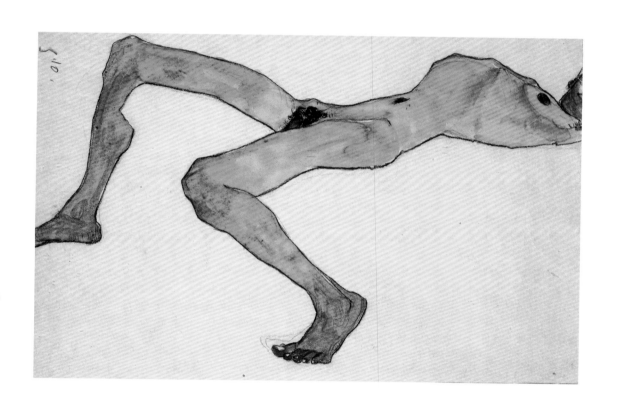

7. SEATED MALE NUDE, 1910.
8. RECLINING MALE NUDE, 1910.

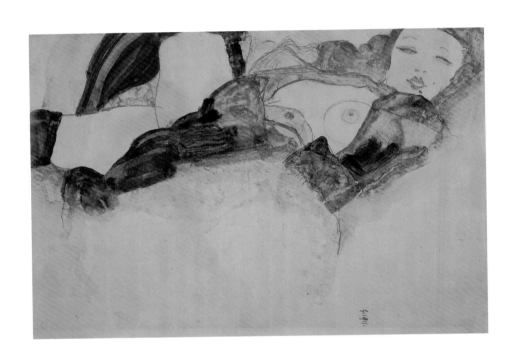

9. RECLINING WOMAN, 1911.
10. THE RED HOST, 1911.

11. STANDING FEMALE NUDE, ARMS CROSSED OVER HER HEAD, 1911.
12. GIRL WITH ELBOW RAISED, 1911.

13. SEATED GIRL WITH RAISED LEFT LEG, 1911.
14. SEATED NUDE GIRL WITH ARMS RAISED OVER HEAD, 1911.

15. NUDE WITH RED GARTERS, 1911.

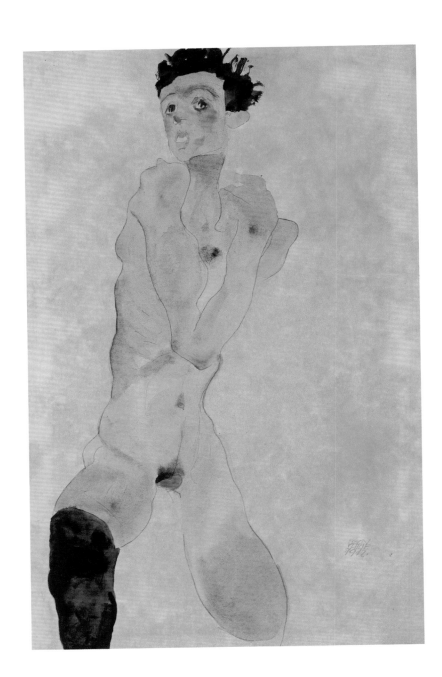

16. STANDING MALE NUDE WITH CROSSED ARMS (SELF-PORTRAIT), 1912.
17. CROUCHING NUDE IN SHOES AND DARK STOCKINGS, BACK VIEW, 1912.

18. RECLINING FEMALE NUDE, 1912.
19. WOMAN WITH RAISED SKIRT, 1913.

20. GIRLFRIEND, PINK-BLUE, 1913.

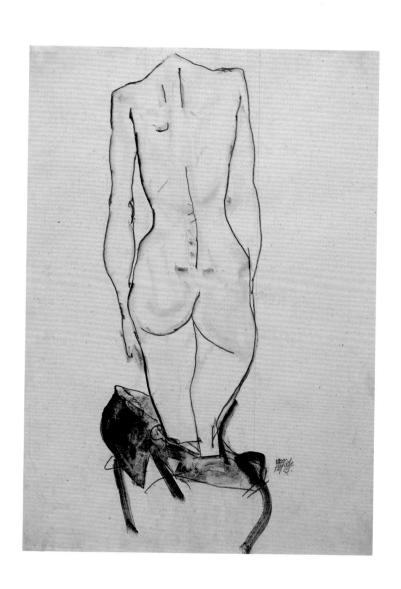

21. STANDING GIRL IN BLUE DRESS AND GREEN STOCKINGS, BACK VIEW, 1913.
22. FEMALE NUDE, BACK VIEW, 1913.

23. STANDING NUDE. 1913.
24. NUDE WITH GREEN TURBAN. 1914.

25. KNEELING NUDE, FRONT VIEW, 1914.
26. SEATED NUDE, 1914.

27. SQUATTING WOMAN, 1914.
28. STANDING NUDE WITH CLOTH, 1917.

29. TWO NUDES (TWO GIRLS), 1917.
30. SEMI-NUDE WITH GREEN STOCKINGS FROM THE BACK, 1917.

31. WOMAN WITH SLIPPER, 1917.
32. TWO GIRLS, 1917.

12.

33. TWO FIGURES, 1917.
34. FEMALE NUDE WITH STOCKINGS, BACK VIEW, 1918.

35. STANDING NUDE GIRL, 1918.
36. SEATED NUDE GIRL CLASPING HER LEFT KNEE, 1918.

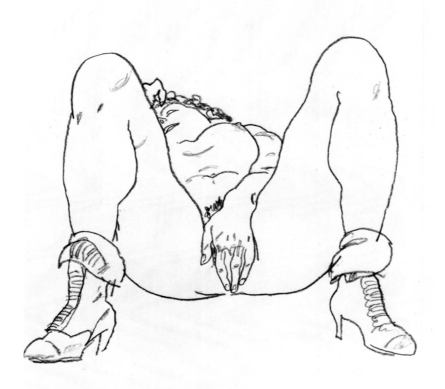

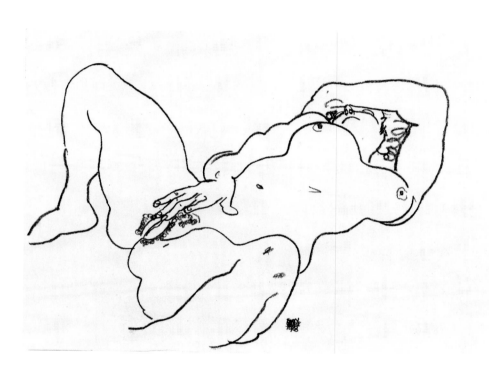

37. RECLINING NUDE WITH BOOTS, 1918.
38. RECLINING NUDE, 1918.

39. RECLINING FEMALE NUDE, 1918.

List of Works
in the Exhibition

NUDE BOY

1906. Charcoal with white heightening on paper, $11\frac{1}{2}$ x $17\frac{1}{2}$ inches (29.2 x 44.5 cm)

Private Collection

SEATED MALE NUDE

1908. Pencil on paper, $12\frac{1}{4}$ x $17\frac{3}{4}$ inches (31 x 45.1 cm)

Private Collection, Vienna

• MOTHER AND CHILD

Plate 1.

1909. Colored crayon and pencil on paper, $5\frac{3}{4}$ x $2\frac{5}{8}$ inches (14.6 x 6.7 cm)

Private Collection

• KNEELING GIRL, DISROBING

Plate 2.

1910. Gouache, watercolor and pencil on paper, $17\frac{5}{8}$ x $12\frac{1}{4}$ inches (44.8 x 31 cm)

Private Collection

• SEATED MALE NUDE

Plate 3.

1910. Watercolor and charcoal on paper, $17\frac{5}{8}$ x $12\frac{1}{4}$ inches (44.7 x 31.2 cm)

Private Collection

• NEWBORN BABY

Plate 4.

1910. Gouache, watercolor and black crayon on paper, $16\frac{5}{8}$ x $11\frac{1}{8}$ inches (42.4 x 28.3 cm)

Private Collection

- STANDING NUDE, BACK VIEW
  Plate 5.
  1910. Gouache, watercolor and pencil with white heightening on paper, 22 x 13 inches (56 x 33.1 cm)
  Private Collection

- FEMALE TORSO
  Plate 6.
  1910. Gouache, watercolor and black crayon with white heightening on paper, 17 $^5/_8$ x 11 $^7/_8$ inches (44.7 x 30.2 cm)
  Private Collection

- SEATED MALE NUDE
  Plate 7.
  1910. Gouache, watercolor and charcoal on paper, 17 $^7/_8$ x 12 $^1/_4$ inches (45.5 x 31.1 cm)
  Private Collection

- RECLINING MALE NUDE
  Plate 8.
  1910. Watercolor and black crayon on paper, 11 $^3/_4$ x 17 $^1/_2$ inches (29.7 x 44.5 cm)
  Private Collection

  SEATED WOMAN WITH RAISED SKIRT
  1910. Pencil on paper, 17 $^1/_2$ x 12 $^5/_8$ inches (44.5 x 32 cm)
  Private Collection

- RECLINING WOMAN
  Plate 9.
  1911. Gouache and pencil on paper, 12 $^3/_8$ x 17 $^3/_8$ inches (31.5 x 44 cm)
  Private Collection

- THE RED HOST
  Plate 10.
  1911. Watercolor and pencil on paper, 19 x 11 $^1/_8$ inches (48.2 x 28.2 cm)
  Private Collection, Courtesy Galerie St. Etienne, New York

- STANDING FEMALE NUDE, ARMS CROSSED OVER HER HEAD
  Plate 11.
  1911. Pencil on paper, 17 x 11 $^7/_8$ inches (43.2 x 30.2 cm)
  Private Collection

- GIRL WITH ELBOW RAISED
  Plate 12.
  1911. Watercolor and pencil on paper, 18 $^7/_8$ x 11 $^3/_4$ inches (47.9 x 29.7 cm)
  Judy and Michael Steinhardt Collection

- SEATED GIRL WITH RAISED LEFT LEG
  Plate 13.
  1911. Gouache, watercolor and pencil on paper, 17 $^1/_2$ x 12 $^1/_8$ inches (44.5 x 30.8 cm)
  Private Collection

- SEATED NUDE GIRL WITH ARMS
  RAISED OVER HEAD
  Plate 14.
  1911. Pencil and watercolor on paper,
  19 x 12 $^3/_8$ inches (48.2 x 31.4 cm)
  Private Collection, London

- NUDE WITH RED GARTERS
  Plate 15.
  1911. Watercolor and pencil on paper,
  21 $^1/_2$ x 14 inches (54.6 x 35.6 cm)
  Private Collection

  FEMALE NUDE
  1911. Gouache, watercolor and pencil on paper,
  21 $^1/_2$ x 14 $^3/_8$ inches (54.6 x 36.5 cm)
  Private Collection

  SEATED FEMALE NUDE
  1911. Pencil on paper, 16 x 11 $^3/_8$ inches
  (40.5 x 29 cm)
  Private Collection, Courtesy Galerie St. Etienne, New York

  STANDING NUDE GIRL
  1911. Pencil on paper, 19 $^3/_4$ x 13 $^3/_8$ inches
  (50.2 x 34 cm)
  Private Collection

- STANDING MALE NUDE WITH
  CROSSED ARMS (SELF-PORTRAIT)
  Plate 16.
  1912. Watercolor and ink on paper,
  18 $^1/_4$ x 11 $^3/_4$ inches (46.4 x 29.8 cm)
  Private Collection

- CROUCHING NUDE IN SHOES AND
  DARK STOCKINGS, BACK VIEW
  Plate 17.
  1912. Gouache, watercolor and pencil on paper,
  19 $^1/_4$ x 12 $^5/_8$ inches (48.9 x 32 cm)
  The Metropolitan Museum of Art, Bequest of Scofield Thayer, 1982

- RECLINING FEMALE NUDE
  Plate 18.
  1912. Pencil on paper, 19 $^3/_4$ x 11 $^3/_4$ inches
  (50.2 x 29.8 cm)
  Private Collection, Vienna

  WOMAN WITH SKIRTS BLOWING
  IN THE WIND
  1912. Watercolor and pencil on paper,
  19 x 12 $^1/_2$ inches (48.2 x 31.7 cm)
  Private Collection, London

  STANDING NUDE WITH WHITE
  DRAPERY
  1912. Gouache, watercolor and pencil on paper,
  19 x 12 $^1/_4$ inches (48.2 x 31 cm)
  Private Collection

- WOMAN WITH RAISED SKIRT
Plate 19.
1913. Watercolor and pencil on paper,
18 ³/₄ x 11 ⁵/₈ inches (47.6 x 29.5 cm)
Private Collection

- GIRLFRIEND, PINK-BLUE
Plate 20.
1913. Gouache, watercolor and black crayon
on paper, 18 ⁷/₈ x 12 ⁵/₈ inches (48 x 32 cm)
Private Collection

- STANDING GIRL IN BLUE DRESS
AND GREEN STOCKINGS, BACK VIEW
Plate 21.
1913. Watercolor and pencil on paper,
18 ¹/₂ x 12 ¹/₄ inches (47 x 31 cm)
Private Collection, California

- FEMALE NUDE, BACK VIEW
Plate 22.
1913. Watercolor and pencil on paper,
18 x 12 ¹/₄ inches (45.7 x 31.1 cm)
*Courtesy Des Moines Art Center Permanent Collection,
Gift of Serge Sabarsky, New York*

- STANDING NUDE
Plate 23.
1913. Pencil on paper, 18 ³/₄ x 12 ³/₈ inches
(47.6 x 31.4 cm)
Estate of Katherine Canaday

SEATED FEMALE NUDE
1913. Pencil on paper, 15 ³/₈ x 8 ⁷/₈ inches
(54.6 x 36.5 cm)
Private Collection

SEATED WOMAN WITH BARE THIGHS
1913. Pencil on paper, 17 ¹/₂ x 11 ⁷/₈ inches
(44.5 x 30.2 cm)
Private Collection, New York

- NUDE WITH GREEN TURBAN
Plate 24.
1914. Gouache and pencil on paper,
12 ⁵/₈ x 18 ⁷/₈ inches (32 x 48 cm)
Private Collection

- KNEELING NUDE, FRONT VIEW
Plate 25.
1914. Pencil on paper, 18 ³/₄ x 12 ³/₈ inches
(47.5 x 31.5 cm)
Private Collection

- SEATED NUDE
Plate 26.
1914. Pencil on paper, 17 ⁷/₈ x 11 ¹/₄ inches
(45.5 x 28.5 cm)
Private Collection

- SQUATTING WOMAN
  Plate 27.
  1914. Drypoint on paper, 19 x 12 $^5/_8$ inches
  (48.3 x 32.2 cm)
  Private Collection

  EMBRACING COUPLE
  1914. Black crayon on paper, 19 $^1/_2$ x 12 $^7/_8$ inches
  (49.5 x 32.7 cm)
  Private Collection

  WOMAN IN UNDERCLOTHES WITH
  RAISED RIGHT ARM
  1914. Black crayon on paper, 18 $^3/_4$ x 12 $^3/_8$ inches
  (47.5 x 31.5 cm)
  Private Collection

- STANDING NUDE WITH CLOTH
  Plate 28.
  1917. Gouache and pencil on paper,
  18 x 11 $^1/_2$ inches (45.7 x 29.3 cm)
  Private Collection, New York

- TWO NUDES (TWO GIRLS)
  Plate 29.
  1917. Black crayon on paper, 11 $^3/_4$ x 17 $^3/_4$ inches
  (29.8 x 45.1 cm)
  Private Collection

- SEMI-NUDE WITH GREEN
  STOCKINGS, FROM THE BACK
  Plate 30.
  1917. Gouache and black crayon on paper,
  18 $^1/_8$ x 11 $^5/_8$ inches (46.1 x 29.5 cm)
  Private Collection

- WOMAN WITH SLIPPER
  Plate 31.
  1917. Charcoal on paper, 11 $^3/_4$ x 18 inches
  (29.8 x 45.7 cm)
  Museum of Modern Art, New York, Gift of Dr. and Mrs. Otto Kallir

- TWO GIRLS
  Plate 32.
  1917. Black crayon on paper, 18 x 11 $^5/_8$ inches
  (45.7 x 29.6 cm)
  Courtesy Alice Adam, Chicago

- TWO FIGURES
  Plate 33.
  1917. Watercolor and charcoal on paper,
  17 $^3/_8$ x 11 $^1/_8$ inches (44.1 x 28.3 cm)
  Collection Walker Art Center, Minneapolis, Gift of Elizabeth and Donald Winston, 1973

  TWO FIGURES, INTERLOCKED
  1917. Black crayon on paper, 18 x 11 $^1/_2$ inches
  (45.7 x 29.2 cm)
  Private Collection

Selected
Chronology

Extracted from *Egon Schiele: The Complete Works*
by Jane Kallir, with permission of the author

1890   Born June 12 to Marie and Adolf Schiele, his father a railway stationmaster in Tulln on the Danube, Austria. The third of four children, Schiele's childhood is marked by illness, perhaps attributable to his father's untreated syphilis at the time of Egon's conception.

1896-   Schiele attends primary and grammar
1902   schools, where his academic performance is unremarkable, except for a prodigious talent for drawing.

1897   Gustav Klimt founds the Secessionist movement in 1897 with a like-minded group of artists and craftsmen; they set no dogmatic aesthetic philosophy, other than to unify the practical and fine arts.

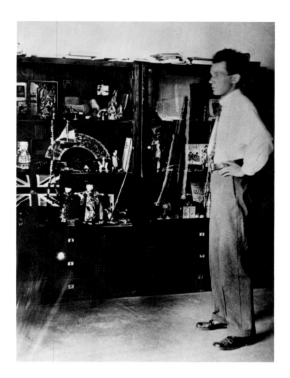

1903   Josef Hoffman and Koloman Moser found the Wiener Werkstätte as a crafts collective intended to formally unify the applied and fine arts as perceived by the Secessionists.

1905   After a period of syphilitic mental illness, his father dies, leaving the family penniless. Schiele completes his first self-portraits.

1906   Academically failing in the Gymnasium in Klosterneuburg, Schiele is asked to withdraw. He passes a difficult entrance exam for the Academy of Fine Arts in Vienna, and with his mother and sister moves there. At the Academy Schiele rebels against his conservative professors and is influenced by Gustav Klimt.

1909   Klimt invites Schiele to exhibit in the international "Kunstschau." Emboldened by this move, Schiele and fellow classmates form the Neukunstgruppe ("New Art Group") and issue a letter of protest against Christian Griepenkerl, their reactionary painting instructor. Schiele and the Neukunstgruppe are forced to withdraw from the Academy, and subsequently stage their first public exhibition. Schiele meets the influential critic Arthur Roessler, who would become an ardent supporter and patron.

INSET: EGON SCHIELE IN FRONT OF HIS DISPLAY CABINET, N.D.

1910   Schiele's work develops at a remarkable pace, and he wins the continued support of both Klimt and the Wiener Werkstätte for his original Expressionist elaborations. Schiele writes his first poems and pursues the theme of nudes.

1911   Quitting Vienna for reasons of love, artistic disputes and the military, Schiele settles in Krumau with Klimt's former model, Wally Neuzil. He befriends Erwin Osen, an eccentric stage designer, painter and avant-garde poseur. His unconventional lifestyle forces him to flee Krumau for nearby Neulengbach.

1912   As a result of his using children as models, he is arrested for kidnapping, statutory rape and public immorality. The first two charges are dropped as unfounded, but he serves twenty-four days in prison on the remaining charge. Returns to Vienna.

1913   Schiele joins the Bund Österreichischer Künstler (Federation of Austrian Artists), and participates in important group exhibitions in Budapest, Cologne, Dresden, Munich, Paris and Rome. Despite financial strains and emotional despondency from official harrassment, Schiele's artistic fame grows, and he enjoys limited but important patronage.

1914   Outbreak of the First World War.

1915   Schiele breaks with Wally Neuzil and marries Edith Harms on June 17th. Three days later he is inducted into the Austrain army and is stationed in Prague.

1916   Schiele is transferred to duty as a guard in a prisoner of war camp at Mühling, Austria. Stationed outside the battle zone, he is allowed to be joined by his wife and is given the use of an empty storeroom as a studio. Although the war disrupts his output and sales, he receives increased recognition when the Berlin periodical *Die Aktion* devotes an entire issue to his work.

1917   Schiele is transferred to the Military Supply Depot in Vienna. His fortunes improve, as the Staatsgalerie in Vienna purchases three of his drawings, and the director, Franz Martin Haberditzl, sits for a major portrait. Schiele organizes a "War Exhibition" which opens in Vienna and travels to Holland, Sweden and Denmark.

1918   Schiele is transferred to the Army Museum in Vienna. The majority of Schiele's fifty works in the new Vienna Secession exhibition are sold. Commissions for portraits increase, and he acquires a new studio. Following the death of Gustav Klimt, Schiele assumes the mantle of Austria's leading progressive artist. Schiele tries to preserve Klimt's studio as a museum. Persistent shortages of food and fuel weaken Schiele and his pregnant wife; both succumb to the influenza epidemic ravaging central Europe. Edith dies on October 28th, followed by the death of Egon on October 31st. Both are buried in the churchyard at Ober St. Veit, Vienna.

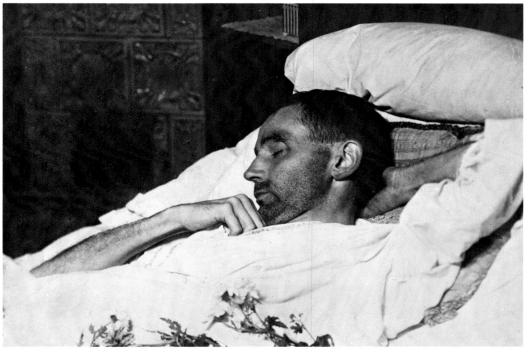

ABOVE: EGON SCHIELE CIRCA 1918; BELOW: SCHIELE ON HIS DEATHBED, 1918.

Published in the United States of America by
Rizzoli International Publications, Inc.
300 Park Avenue South, New York, New York 10010
in association with Gagosian Gallery, New York.
First published on the occasion of the exhibition
EGON SCHIELE: NUDES
from 10 March to 16 April 1994
at Gagosian Gallery

FRONTISPIECE:
Schiele Before His Great Standing Mirror, 1916.
Photograph by Johannes Fischer

All photographs of the artist courtesy Alessandra
Comini and Galerie St. Etienne

Copyright © 1994 Gagosian Gallery
Essay © 1994 Alessandra Comini
Gagosian Gallery project coordinators:
Robert Pincus-Witten, Melissa Lazarov,
Raymond Foye, Lorinda Ash, Philippa Cohen
and Melissa McGrath Mahanes
Design: Anthony McCall Associates, New York

Printed and bound in Italy